YEARS A, B, & C

# Joyful

## Meditations

for

**Every Day
of Advent**

and the

**12 Days
of Christmas**

*Rev. Warren J. Savage*

*Mary Ann McSweeny*

Liguori

ONE LIGUORI DRIVE
LIGUORI MO 63057-9999

Imprimi Potest: Thomas D. Picton, C.Ss.R.
Provincial, Denver Province, The Redemptorists

Published by Liguori Publications
Liguori, Missouri 63057, USA
To order, call 800-325-9521, or visit www.liguori.org.

**Library of Congress Cataloging-in-Publication Data**
Savage, Warren J.
    Joyful meditations for every day of Advent and the 12 days of
Christmas / Warren J. Savage and Mary Ann McSweeny. — 1st ed.
        p. cm.
    ISBN 978-0-7648-1940-7
    1. Advent—Prayers and devotions. 2. Christmas—Prayers and
devotions. I. McSweeny, Mary Ann. II. Title.
    BV40.S29 2010
    242'.33—dc22

                                                        2010020554

Liguori Publications, a nonprofit corporation, is an apostolate of
the Redemptorists. To learn more about the Redemptorists, visit
Redemptorists.com.

Printed in the United States of America
14 13 12 11 10     5 4 3 2 1
First edition

# Contents

# Introduction

The universal church begins a new liturgical year on the first Sunday of Advent. We are called to be God's holy people, waiting in hope and joy for the coming of Christ our Savior. During Advent we proclaim in our lives that hope and joy are gifts from God that make all things new.

Christian joy is the constant awareness of the loving presence of Jesus, the Son of God, in our hearts. Advent is a time when we open our minds and hearts to search for the light of love, compassion, and peace in the Word of God. It is a time set aside for a more intentional reading of the Word of God that leads to personal reflection, prayer, contemplation, and humble service to others. The Advent season challenges us to remove the barriers of arrogance, sadness, selfishness, and greed that hinder us from welcoming Christ with joy and living in communion with him and our brothers and sisters.

There are many people and places in the world waiting to experience joy and good news of better days to come. Joy comes when the darkness of violence and war has been taken away. Joy comes when there is some relief from the pain and suffering that drains the life out of people. Advent makes us aware of our need to participate in God's universal plan for unity. Christians can find great joy in serving others from a place of gratitude for all that is given to us in Jesus Christ, the face of God's joy among us.

These short passages from Scripture, reflections, prayers, and practices for Advent and Christmas offer an opportunity for us to enter more deeply into the mystery of the triune God and increase our longing for the coming of Christ, who is our hope, joy, and peace.

# Advent

# First Sunday of Advent

## YEAR A

---

*Isaiah 2:1–5*
*Psalm 122:1–2, 3–4, 4–5, 6–7, 8–9*
*Romans 13:11–14*
*Matthew 24:37–44*

**One nation shall not raise the sword against another, nor shall they train for war again.**

ISAIAH 2:4B

*Reflection:* There is no joy when we are fighting against one another. There is no joy when we are unwilling to forgive those who have hurt us. There is no joy when our family members and friends have betrayed us. There is no joy when we reject others because of their race, color, culture, ethnic origin, socioeconomic background, gender, sexual orientation, religious tradition, and way of life. Joy comes when we seek the way of peace and love together, when we are intentional in serving the needs of the poor and rebuilding broken lives and families. Joy comes when we can trust and care for each other out of the belief that every person is created in the image of God. Joy comes when we accept all people with a deep sense of respect. Joy comes when the fear of being overpowered and mistreated by others is replaced with true peace, forgiveness, and reconciliation.

**Ponder:** Who or what is robbing me of deep joy and peace in life?

**Prayer:** Lord, give me the courage to disarm my heart from the feelings of anger, resentment, and revenge that foster so much pain and division in my life. Instill within me a spirit of gratitude and joy that I may become your instrument of peace and reconciliation wherever and whenever conflicts arise.

**Practice:** Today I will strive to be a person of joy and peace.

# YEAR B

---

*Isaiah 63:16–17, 19; 64:2–7*
*Psalm 80:2–3, 15–16, 18–19*
*1 Corinthians 1:3–9*
*Mark 13:33–37*

**Yet, O LORD, you are our father; we are the clay and you the potter: we are all the work of your hands.**

ISAIAH 64:7

*Reflection:* It is so easy to forget who made us and continues to love us throughout all the moments of our existence on this earth. We become estranged from God, our Creator, when we place our lives in the hands of the marketplace where life is defined by the restaurants we eat at, the places we buy things, the type of car we drive, the neighborhood we live in, the college we attend, the career and company we work for, the stocks we possess, the elite clubs and organizations to which we belong, and the exotic places where we spend our vacations. We can get lost in the material world and forfeit our relationship with God.

So much of life is caught up in creating a certain image so that others will notice us and accept us. We find it much easier to place our lives in the hands of those who can make our outward appearance look good. It is far more challenging to surrender our lives to our Creator, opening the inner world of our hearts to be transformed by the joy, love, compassion, and peace of God. Yet joy is rekindled when we focus our time and energy on becoming more and more like the image of God in the world.

**Ponder:** What excuses do I give for not spending more time with God?

**Prayer:** Lord, I have become distracted by the things of this world. Guide my steps and lead me safely back home to you. Help me to respond to the needs of others.

**Practice:** Today I will find time to pray and reflect and make God the focus of my attention.

# YEAR C

Jeremiah 33:14–16
Psalm 25:4–5, 8–9, 10, 14
1 Thessalonians 3:12–4:2
Luke 21:25–28, 34–36

"Beware that your hearts do not become drowsy from carousing and drunkenness and the anxieties of daily life, and that day catch you by surprise like a trap. For that day will assault everyone who lives on the face of the earth. Be vigilant...and pray [for] the strength to escape the tribulations that are imminent and to stand before the Son of Man."

LUKE 21:34–36

*Reflection:* The heart is the center of our lives. It is where God chooses to dwell in us and speak to us. It is hard to feel God's presence within us when we are preoccupied with such concerns as paying bills, shopping for food and clothing, keeping social commitments and personal obligations, watching our favorite television shows, and taking care of the family, the home, and the car.

Finding time to be alone with God is not easy because our inner world is weighed down with overwhelming anxiety and sadness. In the midst of our running around taking care of so many things, we lose focus of what is really important in life: our relationship with God. Our lives can become addicted to being busy, but "busy" doesn't equal a healthy, holy life.

God is calling us to slow down, to pay attention and listen to the sounds of joy, love, compassion, and peace deep within us that set us free from the material world's traps. Life is more meaningful and joyful when we live each moment with an attentive heart.

**Ponder:** What am I allowing to overwhelm me, filling my heart with stress and anxiety?

**Prayer:** Lord, help me to slow down and become more aware of my rushing aimlessly from place to place. Quiet my mind and steady my heart that I may live in your presence throughout the day.

**Practice:** Today I will work on doing less in order to be more present to others.

# First Week of Advent

## MONDAY

---

*Isaiah 4:2–6 (A) or Isaiah 2:1–5 (B or C)*
*Psalm 122:1–2, 3–9*
*Matthew 8:5–11*

When [Jesus] entered Capernaum, a centurion approached him and appealed to him, saying, "Lord, my servant is lying at home paralyzed, suffering dreadfully." He said to him, "I will come and cure him."

MATTHEW 8:5–7

**Reflection:** Suffering is not always optional. Life's circumstances can at times paralyze us despite our best efforts. In this numb spiritual state, we suffer and experience distress. The source of our distress may be easily identifiable: we might experience suffering from the effects of divorce or separation, from a loved one's addiction, from pain or illness, from being out of work, or from the death of someone dear to us.

Sometimes the source of our distress eludes us because we are in denial and our suffering may increase because we are unable to accept it.

Turning to God in our distress is the remedy for our suffering. Our need for God, expressed in our plea for relief from the suffering we endure, reconnects us to the source of all life and love and eases our spiritual paralysis. As we open our minds and hearts to God, we learn to trust in God's abiding presence and desire to heal us. We surrender our pride, our feeling that we must bear our burden alone, and we admit our dependence on God.

**Ponder:** What is the source of my pain or suffering that needs God's healing touch?

**Prayer:** Lord, I am in distress and need your loving presence. I ask for your gentle touch that I may be healed and live life with a joy-filled and whole heart.

**Practice:** Today I will make the effort to visit someone who is sick, lonely, or dejected and bring them comfort.

# First Week of Advent

## TUESDAY

---

*Isaiah 11:1–10*
*Psalm 72:1–2, 7–8, 12–13, 17*
*Luke 10:21–24*

**[Jesus] rejoiced in the Holy Spirit.**

LUKE 10:21

*Reflection:* Our baptism has joined us in an intimate bond with the community of God. Father, Son, and Holy Spirit teach us the meaning of interdependence rooted in unconditional love. God's outpouring of love gives us Jesus. Jesus' outpouring of love confirms our true nature as beloved children of God. The Spirit's outpouring of love guides us each day as we struggle to live and love according to Jesus' example.

Although faith assures us that the Spirit is always with us, it may take time for us to be aware of and trust the Spirit's presence and movement in our lives. Whatever rouses our enthusiasm and interest comes from the Spirit. Whenever we speak out in defense of the poor, abused, neglected, or abandoned, we know the Spirit is providing us with the right words. Whenever we share our gifts, talents, and possessions with those in need, we are responding to the prompting of the Spirit. Whenever we forgive those who have hurt us and make amends to those we have hurt, we can trust the Spirit is guiding us.

Recognizing the Spirit's constant movement in our lives deepens our experience of intimacy with the triune God. As we rejoice in the unconditional love of the Father, Son, and Spirit, we are able in our turn to pour out love and compassion into our families, communities, and world.

*Ponder:* Where in my life do I need the help and strength of the Spirit?

*Prayer:* Lord, teach me to open my eyes, ears, and heart that I may rejoice in your Holy Spirit. May your unconditional love strengthen me to live in peace with all people.

*Practice:* Today I will pray for a Spirit of discernment before making important decisions.

# First Week of Advent

## WEDNESDAY

---

*Isaiah 25:6–10a*
*Psalm 23:1–3a, 3b–4, 5, 6*
*Matthew 15:29–37*

**Jesus summoned his disciples and said, "My heart is moved with pity for the crowd, for they have been with me now for three days and have nothing to eat. I do not want to send them away hungry, for fear they may collapse on the way."**

**MATTHEW 15:32**

*Reflection:* God knows our whole self—physical, mental, emotional, and spiritual. God knows we need attention. God knows we need food, clothing, water, and shelter. God knows we need money to pay our bills. God knows we need to relax and enjoy life. God knows we need to find healthy ways to release our anger, sadness, fear, and shame. God knows we need to feel loved and to express the deep love inside us.

We can trust that God will feed us when our human and spiritual needs are unfulfilled. We may have developed the habit of being self-sufficient, thinking we can meet our own needs. We may have been taught that if we want something we must earn it or do it ourselves. Yet the compassion of God anticipates our needs and longs to fulfill them. Often it is through the kindness of people—friends or strangers—that God's compassion comes to us.

**Ponder:** When have I experienced the compassion of God?

**Prayer:** Lord, I am hungry for so much. Teach me to trust that you are meeting my every need. Bless me with the compassion to reach out to others who are physically and spiritually hungry.

**Practice:** Today I will bring canned goods to a local food pantry.

# First Week of Advent

## THURSDAY

_____

*Isaiah 26:1–6*
*Psalm 118:1, 8–9, 19–21, 25–27a*
*Matthew 7:21, 24–27*

"Everyone who listens to these words of mine and acts on them will be like a wise man who built his house on rock. The rain fell, the floods came, and the winds blew and buffeted the house. But it did not collapse; it had been set solidly on rock."

MATTHEW 7:24–25

*Reflection:* The human experience holds no guarantees for physical, mental, or emotional safety. Oftentimes we think a healthy savings account or a good retirement portfolio will give us a feeling of security. Yet unhappiness, disappointment, and anxiety rain on us throughout our lives. Floods of fear, greed, and betrayal can overtake us at any time. Pain, rejection, and death come unexpectedly and blow us off course.

When we surrender our lives and will to the care of our loving Creator, we strengthen our spiritual foundation. Deepening our trust in God's care and compassion for all humanity brings us to the knowledge that all will be well, no matter what challenges our human experience is bringing.

*Ponder:* What do I need to surrender to God today?

*Prayer:* Lord, I long to feel secure and at peace. Let your love be my refuge. Show me how to build my life on the everlasting rock of your compassion.

*Practice:* Today I will make a donation to an organization that helps the poor.

# First Week of Advent

## FRIDAY

———

*Isaiah 29:17–24*
*Psalm 27:1, 4, 13–14*
*Matthew 9:27–31*

**Jesus said to them: "Do you believe that I can do this?"**

**MATTHEW 9:28**

*Reflection:* We know God has the power to do anything. Yet we often find it difficult to believe God can and wants to do things for us.

Somehow over the course of our journey, we have developed a belief that we are unworthy of God's care and compassion. This lack of belief in God's enduring love hinders the Spirit's movement in our lives.

We can change our beliefs. We can affirm our worthiness of God's care and attention. We can ask God to heal our unbelief. We can ask God to show us his will for us. We can pray for the courage and ability to carry out God's will in our interactions with others.

Slowly we relearn the truth of God's unconditional love for us. We experience a deepening intimacy with God. We develop trust that God can, will, and wants to heal us into the joy of eternal love.

**Ponder:** What is God's will for me in this moment?

**Prayer:** Lord, help me to believe I am worthy to be in your loving presence. Bless me with the courage to seek you out, to ask for what I need, and to trust you will answer me.

**Practice:** Today I will have the courage to ask God for help.

# First Week of Advent

## SATURDAY

---

*Isaiah 30:19–21, 23–26*
*Psalm 147:1–2, 3–4, 5–6*
*Matthew 9:35–10:1, 5–8*

**Then [Jesus] said to his disciples: "The harvest is abundant, but the laborers are few; so ask the master of the harvest to send out laborers for his harvest."**

**MATTHEW 9:37–38**

*Reflection:* All of creation is God's harvest, made manifest by the grace of God's love. God's love is boundless, enduring, eternal, abundant, and overflowing. We see signs of this great harvest everywhere: spacious meadows, high mountains, streams of running water, grazing cattle, fields of grain, moonlight, and sunlight.

We see God's harvest most especially in people of all races and cultures who walk many paths with many lifestyles. Artists, janitors, engineers, laborers, firefighters, nurses, doctors, teachers, security guards, secretaries, CEOs, fathers, mothers, children. All of us are laborers of love.

God's love is plentiful because we all have God's love within us. It is up to us to carry on the work of love: to treat all of God's creation with respect, to bring compassion to the brokenhearted, and to nurture those who are wounded and in pain.

**Ponder:** How can I share God's love with one other person today?

**Prayer:** Lord, sometimes I forget that the work of love is my responsibility, too. Help me to join with you to pour out love wherever it is needed.

**Practice:** Today I will take a short, meditative walk in God's creation.

# Second Sunday of Advent

## YEAR A

---

*Isaiah 11:1–10*
*Psalm 72:1–2, 7–8, 12–13, 17*
*Romans 15:4–9; Matthew 3:1–12*

**Even now the ax lies at the root of the trees. Therefore every tree that does not bear good fruit will be cut down and thrown into the fire.**
**MATTHEW 3:10**

***Reflection:*** Genesis tells us that after God created man and woman, God saw everything, and indeed, it was very good. We were made for goodness because God is the source of goodness. We were made to bring forth love because God is the source of love. We were made to be compassionate toward others because God is the source of compassion. We were made to be peacemakers in the world because God is the source of peace. We were made in the image and likeness of God to be God-like wherever we journey in life. We were created to bear good fruit, to show others that we come from God, who is goodness, love, compassion, and peace. Sometimes we forget that we are grounded in divine mystery and not in the ugliness of conflict, hatred, violence, and war. God is patient with us and never abandons us. God gives us time to ground ourselves more deeply in the Word that teaches us to strive to be good, to love our neighbor, to be compassionate to the poor, and to work for peace and justice.

**Ponder:** What is preventing me from believing in my innate goodness and seeing goodness in others?

**Prayer:** Lord, you have created me for goodness, love, compassion, and peace. Help me to make good use of the gifts you have given me to make a difference where I am at this moment of my life.

**Practice:** Today I will affirm my own goodness and look for something good to share with the people around me.

# YEAR B

---

*Isaiah 40:1–5, 9–11*
*Psalm 85:9–10, 11–12, 13–14*
*2 Peter 3:8–14*
*Mark 1:1–8*

**Like a shepherd he feeds his flock; in his arms he gathers the lambs, Carrying them in his bosom, and leading the ewes with care.**

ISAIAH 40:11

*Reflection:* Where is the tenderness and compassion when the world has gone crazy and out of control? We turn our eyes away from the scenes of poor, hungry Haitian children looking for scraps of dirty, rotten food in the garbage pile. We cover our ears because we cannot bear to hear the pained sobbing of a father who just lost his teenage daughter who was killed by another teenager in a drive-by shooting. We refuse to feel the suffering of a young female soldier who lost her legs fighting a war in a foreign country.

We tune out every time we see another person in mental, emotional, spiritual, and physical distress. We do not allow ourselves to be moved to compassion because we are afraid of what it might cost us to become involved in another person's pain and suffering. We choose to remain detached from the human condition and remain isolated in our private world. No matter how desperate things become in life, we can still choose to be like a shepherd and show tenderness and compassion to the poor and vulnerable, and those who are suffering and in pain.

**Ponder:** Why am I afraid to show tenderness and compassion to others?

**Prayer:** Lord, you are the compassion of God in the world. You never forget any of your people. Give me the courage to be the compassion of God for others.

**Practice:** Today I will live with deep awareness and respond with compassion to a troubling situation.

# YEAR C

———

*Baruch 5:1–9*
*Psalm 126:1–2, 2–3, 4–5, 6*
*Philippians 1:4–6, 8–11*
*Luke 3:1–6*

**The LORD has done great things for us; Oh, how happy we were!**

**PSALM 126:3**

*Reflection:* Look around and see! No matter how we feel today, we are blessed with life. We can breathe in the air. We can look up in the sky and see the sun, the moon, and the stars. We can visit the ocean. We can stand by a river or a stream. We can hike in the woods, climb a mountain, or take a scenic ride in the country. We are fortunate to have a place to call our home. We have food to eat, water to drink, clothes for our bodies, and shoes for our feet.

When we stop and reflect for a moment on what we have, we realize how fortunate we are, but there are moments when the thought comes into our minds that we never have enough. Our sense of gratitude and joy disappear. We want more. We think that the more we have, the happier we will be. We need to remember that God has done great things for us, and we can rejoice. We can stand in blessed assurance and gratitude that God is taking good care of us and answers all our needs.

**Ponder:** Why don't I feel satisfied in life?

**Prayer:** Lord, you are always patient with me and do great things for me. Teach me to be more patient in life and grateful for all that has been given to me.

**Practice:** Today I will not complain about anything, but express deep gratitude for everything that comes my way.

# Second Week of Advent

## MONDAY

————

*Isaiah 35:1–10*
*Psalm 85:9ab, 10, 11–12, 13–14*
*Luke 5:17–26*

**"Who but God alone can forgive sins?"**

LUKE 5:21

**Reflection:** We tend to demand perfection according to our own taste, habits, or standards. We often judge others. We criticize others' behavior, actions, words, way of life, style of dress, parenting skills, intelligence, or possessions. We hold on to grudges and resentments and have a hard time letting others be who they are. We make the mistake of thinking we have power to change others.

Yet only God's power can change us. Only God knows where we need healing. Only God knows the deep wounds that distort our thinking and prevent us from loving ourselves and others the way God loves us. Only God has the power to touch our hearts and forgive all that prevents us from being fully human and holy.

Only God knows who we really are. And God loves each of us just as we are, unconditionally, without reservation, and for all eternity.

**Ponder:** Who do I need to forgive?

**Prayer:** Lord, we are all a part of your divine body. When I judge others, I judge myself. Forgive my lack of unconditional love. Show me how to love and accept all people and live with joy.

**Practice:** I will ask God to bless someone I find irritating, threatening, or unworthy of respect.

# Second Week of Advent

## TUESDAY

*Isaiah 40:1–11*
*Psalm 96:1–2, 3, 10ac, 11–12, 13*
*Matthew 18:12–14*

**Comfort, give comfort to my people, says your God.**

ISAIAH 40:1

**Reflection:** Sometimes it seems that life consists of one problem after another. It feels like we have too many burdens to carry and too little energy to bear them. We hear of earthquakes, terrorist attacks, and gang wars, and feel overwhelmed by the anger, violence, and greed that permeate our world. Our personal difficulties seem magnified by these proofs of a troubled and anxious world.

No matter what is going on for us personally or in the world, we can take comfort in knowing God is in charge. God's vision is beyond our understanding. It is a challenge for us to believe that all will be well, but we are called to have hope and to build faith in God's constant love and care for all.

We can help build faith in times of trouble by bringing comfort to others who are anxious, ill, or suffering in any way. A tender word, an expression of gratitude, or an encouraging comment are manifestations of God's love. Acts of kindness and love give us the confidence that God is indeed here among us, ensuring that not one of us is lost to despair.

***Ponder:*** Who has been a source of comfort to me?

***Prayer:*** Lord, give me a positive outlook on life. Help me to lessen the stress and anxiety in the world. May your Spirit empower me to offer comfort rather than complaints; to speak tenderly rather than angrily; to seek your presence rather than wander aimlessly on my own.

***Practice:*** Today I will speak words of gratitude and encouragement to everyone I encounter.

# Second Week of Advent

## WEDNESDAY

---

*Isaiah 40:25–31*
*Psalm 103:1–2, 3–4, 8, 10*
*Matthew 11:28–30*

[Jesus said:] "Take my yoke upon you and learn from me, for I am meek and humble of heart; and you will find rest for your selves."

**MATTHEW 11:29**

***Reflection:*** Humility is the gift of being teachable. Jesus asks us to learn from him, to let him be our teacher. In becoming Jesus' students, we learn to let go of the burdens of arrogance, pride, selfishness, and fear. We learn to treat others and ourselves gently, with respect and courtesy. We learn to build up God's kingdom by speaking positively, encouraging others to develop their talents, and making good use of our own gifts.

By word and example, Jesus teaches us the way to holiness. He teaches us to respond with compassion to the ill, abandoned, and rejected; to help the poor and vulnerable; and to choose mercy over revenge. He teaches us to pray and meditate. He teaches us to listen to and love the Scriptures and to draw strength from them.

Jesus wears a yoke of love. As we take that yoke upon us and seek out Jesus' wisdom, we become more skilled at loving others unconditionally and find that love is never a burden and weighs nothing to carry. Peace and joy are restored when we love God with all our mind, heart, soul, and strength, and our neighbor as ourselves.

*Ponder:* What keeps me from being gentle and humble of heart?

*Prayer:* Lord, I wish to be your faithful disciple. Heal me of the arrogance that prevents me from being teachable. Teach me how to wear the yoke of love.

*Practice:* Today I will walk with a gentle and humble heart.

# Second Week of Advent

## THURSDAY

---

*Isaiah 41:13–20*
*Psalm 145:1, 9, 10–11, 12–13ab*
*Matthew 11:11–15*

**For I am the LORD, your God, who grasps your right hand; It is I who say to you, "Fear not, I will help you."**

ISAIAH 41:13

**Reflection:** Whatever we have experienced in life, whoever has hurt us, however we have failed, wherever we have injured others, God tells us to trust and not to be afraid. God is here to help us find a way out of our confusion and disharmony into a place of serenity and joy.

We have to trust that God will help us transform anger into mercy; selfishness into generosity; rudeness into kindness; conflict into reconciliation; stubbornness into cooperation; indifference into compassion. We have to trust that when we are ill, we are still whole enough to reach out and care for others. We have to trust that our hatred of others can be transformed into love for our neighbor. We have to trust that times of sadness will be turned into moments of great joy and celebration. We have to trust that when we are near death we have been promised the gift of eternal life.

As we experience the richness of life lived with deep trust, we are able to surrender more and more. We become more childlike in our trust of God. We let go of fear and enter into the joy of living. Our example helps others gain confidence to live life fully.

*Ponder:* Who can I trust in a time of need?

*Prayer:* Lord, thank you for walking with me throughout my life. Help me to entrust my life to your loving care. Show me how to enjoy the fruits of your kindness, mercy, and compassion.

*Practice:* Today I will trust my gut and surrender all to God.

# Second Week of Advent

## FRIDAY

———

*Isaiah 48:17–19*
*Psalm 1:1–2, 3, 4, 6*
*Matthew 11:16–19*

**The law of the LORD is their joy; God's law they study day and night.**

**PSALM 1:2**

**Reflection:** When we put God in the center of our lives, we commit to making love the source of our every thought, action, and word. We take responsibility in every moment to choose the way we think, act toward others, and perceive the world. With the love of God, we find the power to change hateful thinking into positive insights and disrespect of others into acts of kindness, encouragement, and support.

Sometimes we fail to make God's love the source and delight of our lives. We would rather be consumed by text messages, computer games, and television and obsessed by shopping, gambling, or working out.

When we meditate on how we live in light of God's love, we discover how arid and meaningless our life has become. We feel disconnected and unfulfilled because we do not allow God's love to touch us. We've avoided the love of others because we've been afraid of responsibility and intimacy. We have lost the ability to delight in life because we have forgotten how to delight in the gift of love.

Although we are human, we must continue to strive to be like God and continue to make progress in the work of love. Life is more delightful when we are detached from the things of the world and focused on loving God, self, and neighbor.

*Ponder:* Is my life focused on the love of God, self, and neighbor?

*Prayer:* Lord, I long to delight in your love. Give me the courage to change hatred to love, conflict to peace, and sadness to joy.

*Practice:* Today I will look back over my day and gently acknowledge where I showed love and where I failed to show love to others.

# Second Week of Advent

## SATURDAY

---

*Sirach 48:1–4, 9–11*
*Psalm 80:2ac, 3b, 15–16, 18–19*
*Matthew 17:9a, 10–13*

**Till like a fire there appeared the prophet whose words were as a flaming furnace.**

**SIRACH 48:1**

*Reflection:* Throughout Scripture we hear stories of the prophets—people who were guided by the Holy Spirit to challenge others to change the social order and seek a life of love, generosity, compassion, and care for the poor.

We, too, have the power to influence others to live according to God's commandment to love. Our life witness may seem unremarkable: nurturing our children, going to work, visiting a sick friend, caring for aging parents, doing our best in school, watching for ways to be helpful or encouraging, putting aside our wants when someone needs our attention, bringing food to the food pantry, providing clothing for those in need. Yet these everyday sacrifices shine a steady light in our world and add up to a prophetic statement of the power of God's love.

We also have the power to bring about change when we speak out against injustice, racism, discrimination, and war, and when we speak up in defense of those who are unborn, poor, without homes, out of work, or seeking refuge. Risking our comfort in order to help others is a prophetic witness to God's ever-present compassion.

*Ponder:* Where do I need to be a prophetic witness today?

*Prayer:* Lord, you give meaning and purpose to my life. Open my eyes to see new opportunities to share your goodness and love in my everyday adventures. Help me to know that sharing and accepting love is your will for me.

*Practice:* Today I will speak up when I hear derogatory comments about other races, cultures, or groups of people.

# Third Sunday of Advent

## YEAR A

---

*Isaiah 35:1–6a, 10*
*Psalm 146:6–7, 8–9, 9–10*
*James 5:7–10*
*Matthew 11:2–11*

**Be patient, therefore, brothers, until the coming of the Lord.**

**JAMES 5:7**

*Reflection:* We seem to grow more impatient with ourselves each day. We don't give ourselves enough time to think things through, to get in touch with our true feelings, to wait for God to answer a special prayer request, and to simply enjoy and savor life.

As we grow more impatient with ourselves, we also grow more impatient with others. We dismiss others because we don't have time to listen to their problems. We are quick to judge others because we have no interest in getting to know them and fostering healthy relationships. We are rude to the waiter or waitress, the bank teller, the cashier at the supermarket, the toll booth attendant, the janitor, and anyone else we just don't have time to deal with.

When we are impatient in life, we can become harsh and bitter toward others. When we are impatient, we deplete the joy and love that is deep within us. When we are impatient, we make others feel uncomfortable and unimportant. When we are impatient we find it difficult to trust, forgive, love, and reconcile our differences. Being patient is an act of love.

*Ponder:* Why am I so impatient in life?

*Prayer:* Lord, you are patient with me and give me time to correct my faults and become a better person. Help me to be more patient and loving toward others.

*Practice:* Today I will be patient and kind toward everyone I encounter.

# YEAR B

---

*Isaiah 61:1–2a, 10–11*
*Luke 1:46–48, 49–50, 53–54*
*1 Thessalonians 5:16–24*
*John 1:6–8, 19–28*

**Rejoice always. Pray without ceasing. In all circumstances give thanks, for this is the will of God for you in Christ Jesus.**

**1 Thessalonians 5:16–18**

***Reflection:*** It is easy to rejoice when life is going well for us. We rejoice when we receive good news; when we receive a special honor or reward; when we win a contest; when we graduate and succeed in life; and when we are the center of attention. It is more difficult to rejoice when life falls on hard times: when we are living with cancer or another disease; when someone close to us dies; when we are unemployed and cannot pay our bills; when we start a recovery program to deal with our addictions; and when we lose faith in God.

Our joy in life is rooted in our relationship with God. We trust that no matter what happens in life, our relationship with God is much stronger and can endure whatever comes our way. Our trust in God's love for us moves us to pray without ceasing. Through prayer we can sense God's presence with us and are able to rejoice in the truth that God saves us and make us whole again.

In times of crisis, our first response is usually to complain rather than to give thanks. Our faith demands a different response. We are to give thanks in all circumstances because God is close to all who are in pain and in need of comfort and peace.

*Ponder:* What am I always complaining about in life?

*Prayer:* Lord, you are the source of my strength, peace, and joy. Send your Spirit to renew my trust and hope in you and give me peace.

*Practice:* Today I will not complain but rejoice in the gift of being alive.

# YEAR C

---

*Zephaniah 3:14–18a*
*Isaiah 12:2–3, 4, 5–6*
*Philippians 4:4–7*
*Luke 3:10–18*

**"Whoever has two cloaks should share with the person who has none. And whoever has food should do likewise."**

**LUKE 3:11**

*Reflection:* Compassion is our ability to feel the pain and suffering of others. It also means seeing ourselves mirrored in those whose lives are fragile and near death because of a lack of food, shelter, clothing, and medical attention. For those who are naked, joy comes when someone, out of a deep sense of compassion, offers them clothes. For those who are hungry, joy comes when a caring person brings them food to eat. For those who wander the streets looking for shelter, joy comes when a community of caring people builds a home for them to live in.

Each day there are people near and far away who await some assistance to better their lives.

They hope and pray that the people with two coats will share, that the people who have more than enough food will not waste what they have but will find it in their hearts to give them something to eat.

Selfish, self-centered persons are not happy persons. There is no joy to be found in a greedy, narcissistic world. There is no joy when those who have more are unwilling to give to those who have nothing to live on.

When compassion is demonstrated in real ways such as giving clothes to the needy, building homes for the homeless, and collecting food for the poor in our communities, joy is rediscovered and celebrated.

**Ponder:** How much do I waste in life? What can I give to eliminate local and global poverty?

**Prayer:** Lord, you are generous and kind to all your people. Instill within me a compassionate and generous heart that I may respond to my poor sisters and brothers near and far away.

**Practice:** Today I will gather food supplies and bring them to a local food bank.

# Third Week of Advent

## MONDAY

*Numbers 24:2–7, 15–17a*
*Psalm 25:4–5ab, 6–7bc, 8–9*
*Matthew 21:23–27*

**When [Jesus] had come into the temple area, the chief priests and the elders of the people approached him as he was teaching and said, "By what authority are you doing these things? And who gave you this authority?"**

**MATTHEW 21:23**

*Reflection:* God is our authority. God gives us the right to be who we are: human, lovable, loving, precious children of God. No one has the right to tell us otherwise.

Sometimes in our church, community, workplaces, or families, others will try to undermine our sense of worthiness and rob us of our human dignity. This is an effort to render us powerless, an effort to control us. God gives us the authority to reject all efforts to shame or manipulate us.

Even if we are not skillful at expressing ourselves, God gives us the authority to speak from our hearts to share our wisdom, experience, and faith. God gives us the authority to question those who claim to be authorities. God gives us the authority to choose a different path from a way we feel is not in keeping with God's command to love.

When we root our lives in prayer and seek God's will in everything we do, we may find others are not comfortable with the authority by which we are living. Yet God has given us this authority, and it is our right and freedom to make use of it.

**Ponder:** How do I express my confidence in God's authority?

**Prayer:** Lord, your authority never intimidates me. May your loving authority guide me to live wisely, lovingly, and in accordance with your will.

**Practice:** Today I will speak out against unjust practices in order that others may not be victimized.

# Third Week of Advent

## TUESDAY

---

*Zephaniah 3:1–2, 9–13*
*Psalm 34:2–3, 6–7, 17–18, 19, 23*
*Matthew 21:28–32*

> [Jesus said to them]: "A man had two sons. He came to the first and said, 'Son, go out and work in the vineyard today.' He said in reply, 'I will not,' but afterwards he changed his mind and went."
>
> **MATTHEW 21:28–29**

**Reflection:** It is never too late to change our minds, our attitudes, or our behaviors. In our hearts we know the will of God; as we become more skilled at listening to our hearts, we may find we need to make changes in how we are living.

It takes courage and humility to change. We may have developed certain habits during our lifetime that are based in fear, shame, or anger. We may have learned to cope with difficult life situations by manipulating others; by becoming addicted to alcohol, food, or gambling; or by letting others define who we are. However, whatever unhealthy patterns we may have acquired, we have the right to be the sons and daughters of God. We have the power to change at any time and live life more freely and lovingly.

**Ponder:** What habits do I need or want to change to live more freely and lovingly?

**Prayer:** Lord, you show me how to be just, compassionate, and generous. May your grace give me the courage I need to change all that prevents me from loving you, myself, and my neighbor.

**Practice:** Today I will take time to think and pray before acting.

# Third Week of Advent

## WEDNESDAY

---

*Isaiah 45:6c–8, 18, 21c–25*
*Psalm 85:9–10ab, 11–12, 13–14*
*Luke 7:18b–23*

And [Jesus] said to them in reply, "Go and tell John what you have seen and heard: the blind regain their sight, the lame walk, lepers are cleansed, the deaf hear, the dead are raised, the poor have the good news proclaimed to them."

**LUKE 7:22**

**Reflection:** Our understanding of God comes from how we experience God. With Jesus, our experience of God is one of healing, hope, and transformation through the power of unconditional love.

Luke's Gospel calls us to look for new ways to bring the experience of God's healing, hope, and love to all those within our sphere of influence. For example, we have the power to heal by sharing forgiveness; we have the power to give hope by lending a helping hand to those who are struggling with illness, joblessness, or aging; we have the power to transform low self-esteem and low self-worth by accepting ourselves and others just as we are without judgment or criticism.

As we bring an experience of God's healing, hope, and unconditional love to our homes, schools, workplaces, and communities, we find that the reality of God's presence becomes easier to recognize in the people around us.

*Ponder:* Where do I need to bring healing, hope, and love in my daily life?

*Prayer:* Lord, you alone are God. Open my eyes, ears, and heart to experience your loving presence as I go through the day. May I seek opportunities to share your healing, hope, and unconditional love with all those I encounter.

*Practice:* Today I will practice unconditional love by accepting myself and others without judgment.

# Third Week of Advent

If today is December 17 or 18, use the readings and reflection for that day.

## THURSDAY

---

*Isaiah 54:1–10*
*Psalm 30:2, 4, 5–6, 11–12a, 13b*
*Luke 7:24–30*

**Sing praise to the LORD, you faithful; give thanks to God's holy name.**

**PSALM 30:5**

*Reflection:* Thanks and praise are natural expressions of our profound gratitude to God. Gratitude lives in our hearts. It arises from a humble awareness of God's boundless love for us just as we are. We want to be like God in goodness and love, and we know that at times we fail out of human frailty. Yet in every moment God helps us to make a fresh start and renews us with the comfort of unconditional love.

Gratitude does not always come naturally. We may have lost faith in God or had our trust broken by people we love; we may feel abandoned and rejected by others and God; we may feel God never answers our prayers. If we look at our lives in complete honesty, however, we can find at least one blessing. We can begin to cultivate gratitude by making a habit of thanking God every day for each blessing we uncover.

**Ponder:** When do I give thanks and praise to God?

**Prayer:** Lord, I give thanks and praise to you for the gift of life. Teach me to be grateful for all that I experience—the joys, challenges, and grief.

**Practice:** Today I will show my awareness of the my life's blessings by saying grace before meals.

# Third Week of Advent

If today is December 17 or 18, use the readings and reflection for that day.

## FRIDAY

---

*Isaiah 56:1–3a, 6–8*
*Psalm 67:2–3, 5, 7–8*
*John 5:33–36*

Thus says the LORD: Observe what is right, do what is just; for my salvation is about to come, my justice, about to be revealed.

ISAIAH 56:1

*Reflection:* We have a deep longing to be perfect in our dealings with others, but our humanity gets in the way. Sometimes we feel stuck and unable to help ourselves. Sometimes we feel like victims of someone or something and indulge in self-pity. Sometimes we get lost in obsessive thinking and can't focus on what we need to do. Sometimes we let tasks and chores pile up until we are overwhelmed and completely stressed out.

Sometimes we take out our anger or frustration on others and act unjustly.

Our best first remedy is prayer. Asking God to show us the next right thing to do helps us to get unstuck, stop feeling sorry for ourselves, find clarity in our thinking, bring order to our lives, and treat others with respect and dignity.

We might need to ask God to show us the next right thing to do a hundred times a day. This kind of conscious contact with God benefits us as we become more and more aware of God's movement in our lives. We begin to trust God is there for us and will always help us find a new way of living.

*Ponder:* How do I maintain justice in my dealings?

*Prayer:* Lord, your ways are just and loving. Help me to turn to you and humbly ask for your guidance so that I may learn to be more like you.

*Practice:* Today I will ask God to know and do what is right and just.

# Fourth Sunday of Advent

## YEAR A

---

*Isaiah 7:10–14*
*Psalm 24:1–2, 3–4, 5–6*
*Romans 1:1–7*
*Matthew 1:18–24*

**"Look, the virgin shall conceive and bear a son, and they shall name him Emmanuel, which means, 'God is with us.'"**

**MATTHEW 1:23**

***Reflection:*** The secular world wants to convince us that we can get along in life without God. There are schools of thought promoting the idea that there is no need to believe in God and that to believe in God is utter foolishness. There are some scholars who believe that they are the masters of their own worlds and that they can find their way to happiness and peace without God. The arrogant and the powerful refute the claim that "God is with us." They are self-autonomous, self-sufficient, and the center of their own world.

Those who recognize their own powerlessness and sense their incompleteness come to believe and trust that "God is with us." They believe in their hearts that there is someone greater to depend on for our existence. They believe that life has a deeper meaning and purpose with God.

God is with us in a variety of ways. God is with us in all of creation. God is with us in the diversity of humanity. God is with us in sacred Scripture, in the Eucharist, in the Church and sacraments, and in all the acts of charity we offer to the poor and needy everywhere.

We can take a valuable lesson from the poor and powerless. In their humble living, they know that "God is with us." They know that they can find the God of joy and peace in their hearts.

**Ponder:** What makes me doubt the truth that God is with us?

**Prayer:** Lord, you are Emmanuel, "God with us." Open the eyes and ears of my heart that I may see your presence in every person I meet, and hear your voice in the cry of the poor.

**Practice:** Today I will be with God by reading and reflecting on Psalm 24.

# YEAR B

---

*2 Samuel 7:1–5, 8b–12; 14a, 16*
*Psalm 89:2–3, 4–5, 27, 29*
*Romans 16:25–27*
*Luke 1:26–38*

**I have been with you wherever you went, and I have destroyed all your enemies before you.**

**2 SAMUEL 7:9A**

*Reflection:* We all have a real or perceived enemy to deal with in life. What would life look like and feel like if there was no longer an enemy to conquer? We would experience peace and joy. There would be a sense of harmony, mutual respect, and understanding.

Each day we are presented with a potential enemy, someone to hate or dislike. We awaken to the news that another suicide bomber blew himself or herself up, killing and injuring people somewhere in the world. We read and hear about the shootings on the streets, in our schools, and even in places of worship. We watch in dismay the removal of the members of a family killed as a result of domestic violence. There seems to be a never-ending stream of images of conflict, war, and violence flooding our minds. We have become numb and indifferent to all the violence around us.

As long as we have an enemy to conquer in life, there will never be peace in the world. We may not be able to resolve all the global wars and conflicts, but we can do our part in the world by reconciling with our enemies and living an intentional life of forgiveness and peace. We are all brothers and sisters, created in the image and likeness of God. It is time to embrace God's vision, to live and rejoice in this truth. It is time to be friends and not enemies.

*Ponder:* Who are the enemies in my life that I need to be reconciled with?

*Prayer:* Lord, you have called us to be your instruments of peace and reconciliation in the world. Give me the courage to make peace with those who have hurt me and caused me pain.

*Practice:* Today I will pray for my enemies and those who persecute me.

# YEAR C

---

*Micah 5:1–4a*
*Psalm 80:2–3, 15–16, 18–19*
*Hebrews 10:5–10*
*Luke 1:39–45*

**"Blessed are you who believed that what was spoken to you by the Lord would be fulfilled."**

LUKE 1:45

***Reflection:*** God speaks to us in the Scriptures about the nature of the kingdom of God, about the power of love and compassion, about mercy and justice, about the way of righteousness and holiness, about the choice between life and death, about the meaning and purpose of suffering, about truth and about faith, hope, and love.

Everything God speaks to us is revealed in a personal way, in Jesus, the Son of God. When we read what Jesus teaches his disciples, we, too, are invited to listen in, to take to heart what Jesus shared with his friends. Like Mary, the first disciple, we are called to ponder the Word of God in our hearts and trust that what the Lord has revealed will be fulfilled in us, in God's time.

Through the practice of *lectio divina* we learn how to take the Word of God and reflect on it. We learn to be patient with God, with ourselves, and with others as we await God's plan to be fulfilled in the world.

As we journey through this life, we need to share the ways in which God is stirring inside us. We need to be able to share our experience of God with others without fear.

**Ponder:** Why am I reluctant to read and reflect on the Word of God each day?

**Prayer:** Lord, your Word gives me life, joy, hope, and peace. May your Word find a home in me and inspire me to live a life rooted in gospel values.

**Practice:** Today I will begin reading and reflecting on the Gospel of Luke.

# December 17
## Through
# December 24

# December 17

*Genesis 49:2, 8–10*
*Psalm 72:1–2, 3–4ab, 7–8, 17*
*Matthew 1:1–17*

**The book of the genealogy of Jesus Christ, the son of David, the son of Abraham.**

**MATTHEW 1:1**

***Reflection:*** From the record of Jesus' genealogy, we learn he is descended from Abraham, who is known as the father of three major religions: Islam, Judaism, and Christianity. Jesus' DNA also matches that of kings, adulterers, godly men and women, a prostitute, and a murderer. Jesus the human person is the offspring of generations of saints and sinners—just as we are.

The genealogy of Jesus also teaches us that Jesus the divine is connected to everyone, regardless of social status, beliefs, or way of life. Jesus is found in everyone and everyone is found in Jesus. As we recognize that the whole of humanity is reflected in Jesus' family, we renew our commitment to treat ourselves and all people with love and respect. We all come from Jesus the Messiah. We are all members of the family of God.

**Ponder:** How does being a member of Jesus' family change my way of living?

**Prayer:** Lord, every human is created in your image and is a sacred member of your family. Forgive me for the times I have ignored, disregarded, or disrespected one of my sisters and brothers.

**Practice:** Today I will explore my family tree.

# December 18

*Jeremiah 23:5–8*
*Psalm 72:1–2, 12–13, 18–19*
*Matthew 1:18–25*

Joseph her husband, since he was a righteous man, yet unwilling to expose her to shame, decided to divorce her quietly. Such was his intention when, behold, the angel of the Lord appeared to him in a dream and said, "Joseph, son of David, do not be afraid to take Mary your wife into your home. For it is through the Holy Spirit that this child has been conceived in her."

**MATTHEW 1:19–20**

*Reflection:* When we have been hurt or betrayed, in our shock and pain we often react without thinking. We might withdraw mentally and emotionally from the situation. We might counter-attack with angry words or hurtful actions. We might seek legal recourse. We might use personal knowledge to bring public disgrace to the one who has hurt us. We want to insist on our rights.

Joseph shows us a new way of responding to the hurtful experiences that come our way. He chooses what he believes is a just solution that will keep Mary safe from public censure and disgrace. Joseph is able to put aside his personal pain to consider Mary's well-being.

Listening deeply for God's guidance in our lives helps us to learn a more forgiving way of being. We may even find ourselves acting in ways that don't seem to make sense according to the way we were brought up or the way our society works. Yet when we base our actions in unconditional love, we can trust that God is with us, leading us every step of the way.

*Ponder:* How do I respond when someone hurts me?

*Prayer:* Lord, give me a humble heart to hear your quiet voice. Teach me to be calm and listen to you so that I may act according to your law of love.

*Practice:* Today I will let go of the need to be right and choose to be loving instead.

# December 19

*Judges 13:2–7, 24–25a*
*Psalm 71:3–4a, 5–6ab, 16–17*
*Luke 1:5–25*

But the angel said to him, "Do not be afraid, Zechariah, because your prayer has been heard."

**LUKE 1:13**

*Reflection:* We pray in many ways. Sometimes we pray to give thanks. Sometimes we pray to ask for help. Sometimes we pray for others. Sometimes we pray for things we really want. Sometimes we pray to tell God our failings. Sometimes we pray without words. Sometimes we cannot pray, and others pray for us.

If we care about what we're praying about, we can trust that God cares, too. We never need to fear that our manner of praying will interfere with our relationship with God. Prayer connects us to God. God hears our prayer, even when we have no way to express ourselves. And God always answers our prayer. In God's time. In God's way. For our highest good.

*Ponder:* How do I pray? How do I know God is listening? When have my prayers been answered?

*Prayer:* Lord, I need so much from you. Help me to know that you are listening and providing me with everything I need today.

*Practice:* Today I will ask God for what I need and then let go in trust that God has heard and is answering.

# December 20

*Isaiah 7:10–14*
*Psalm 24:1–2, 3–4ab, 5–6*
*Luke 1:26–38*

**Mary said, "Behold, I am the handmaid of the Lord. May it be done to me according to your Word."**

**LUKE 1:38**

*Reflection:* We all long to feel we have a particular purpose, a reason for being, a unique place in the world. Mary shows us the simple formula for defining our purpose: Here, in this moment, we must be present to God and ready to serve God according to God's will.

It is not an easy task to keep our focus on the here and now. Yet to cultivate awareness of God's presence, we need to learn to live one moment at a time. Instead of dwelling on the past or projecting what might happen in the future, we can intentionally use all of our senses to be aware of what is happening right now. This awareness opens our hearts to be filled with God's love. As we respond in gratitude, we find our purpose: to serve God by sharing God's love with all of his family.

**Ponder:** How much time do I spend living in the past or the future? What makes it difficult for me to be fully alive in the present moment?

**Prayer:** Lord, keep my mind from useless distractions. Teach me to calm my thoughts, listen to my breath, and be here with you in each moment.

**Practice:** Today I will practice moment-to-moment awareness.

# December 21

*Song of Songs 2:8–14*
*Psalm 33:2–3, 11–12, 20–21*
*Luke 1:39–45*

**When Elizabeth heard Mary's greeting, the infant leaped in her womb.**

**LUKE 1:41**

***Reflection:*** It is our joy and our calling to bring love with us wherever we go. All of us, even the unborn, recognize the voice of love. We know what it is to feel the balm of comforting words, the consolation of reassuring words, and the joy of appreciative words.

We also know what it is to see the face of love. Whenever we light up at the sight of someone, we are seeing our own love reflected in that person. God within us recognizes God within the other person and responds with a leap of joy.

Our challenge is to learn to recognize God within the people who disturb, dismiss, or disrespect us. We can make a start by speaking courteously and appreciatively to those we find it hard to love. We can shine our light of goodness and love in the darkness that we feel in the presence of those who trouble us. We can make an intentional effort to be peacemakers in all situations.

**Ponder:** Where does my inner light shine most brightly? Who is a beacon of love in my life?

**Prayer:** Lord, you offer your love freely to all. Help me to let go of anger, resentment, and pride and let your love shine through me.

**Practice:** Today I will greet and smile at every person I meet.

# December 22

*1 Samuel 1:24–28*
*1 Samuel 2:1, 4–5, 6–7, 8*
*Luke 1:46–56*

[Mary said,] "He has shown might with his arm, dispersed the arrogant of mind and heart."

**LUKE 1:51**

***Reflection:*** Pride is a stumbling block to spiritual wholeness. Pride tells us that we do not need to look deeply at our lives and face the dark parts of ourselves. Pride keeps us from admitting our human failings of selfishness, indifference, prejudice, or greed. Our pride may be so strong that we cannot admit our dependence on God and so we begin to feel that everything depends on us or that we are in charge.

Because of pride, we cannot be vulnerable and open to the healing and compassion God offers us. Pride hinders our ability to know our true nature of love and goodness. Although we might look good on the outside, our inner selves are scattered and desperately seeking the way to wholeness.

It is rarely comfortable to confront our weaknesses. To let go of pride means we must admit we are weak and in need of help. Yet if we have the courage to let go of pride and admit our powerlessness and complete dependence on God, we will find freedom and inner peace.

**Ponder:** Where does pride manifest in my life? When have I become spiritually arrogant? When have I needed God?

**Prayer:** Lord, your presence makes my life whole. Take away my pride so that I have the courage to change the attitudes, habits, and behaviors that prevent me from being more like you.

**Practice:** Today I will volunteer at a soup kitchen.

# December 23

*Malachi 3:1–4, 23–24*
*Psalm 25:4–5ab, 8–9, 10, 14*
*Luke 1:57–66*

**"What, then, will this child be?" For surely the hand of the Lord was with him.**

LUKE 1:66

**Reflection:** There is such hope in the birth of a baby. This new, precious being is a bundle of endless possibilities, a mystery that must be allowed to unfold at its own pace in order to totally manifest its inner truth of love and goodness.

Throughout our lives, we experience change that is, in effect, a rebirth. At every stage of our life we explore new possibilities. We encounter new friends, new schools, new jobs, new family members, new responsibilities, new challenges.

Sometimes the possibilities are frightening. When we remember the hand of the Lord is with us, we can face challenges with faith and courage. We can surrender our disappointments, loss, and physical difficulties to God and ask to be shown the gift within them.

Sometimes the possibilities we face are joyous and exciting, and we more easily recognize the gift within. It is our privilege to seek the hand of the Lord within these gifts, too, and humbly express our gratitude.

All of life is a gift of endless possibilities for sharing and experiencing God's love and goodness. As we dare to explore these endless possibilities, we become more and more like God in compassion, forgiveness, and acceptance.

*Ponder:* What will I become in life? Am I satisfied with my life at the moment? What would I like to accomplish with God's help?

*Prayer:* Lord, all things are possible with you. Help me know my inner truth of love and goodness and manifest this totally in my relations with others.

*Practice:* Today I will write a letter of encouragement to someone I have neglected.

# December 24

*2 Samuel 7:1–5, 8b–12, 14a, 16*
*Psalm 89:2–3, 4–5, 27, 29*
*Luke 1:67–79*

[Zechariah spoke this prophecy:] "[By] the tender mercy of our God,…the daybreak from on high will visit us to shine on those who sit in darkness and death's shadow, to guide our feet into the path of peace."

LUKE 1:78–79

*Reflection:* God wishes us to know the truth of his tender love and care for us. God's light of love shines on us not only to brighten our days, but also to illuminate the dark areas of our hearts that prevent us from walking with God. We know that God's way is the way of love. We know that we are called to love ourselves and our neighbors. Yet sometimes we have difficulty choosing love.

God's merciful light guides us to make needed changes to let go of the wounds, fears, and prejudices that prevent us from following the way of love. As we allow God's light to shine on our hearts, we see more clearly how beloved each of us is; what gentle creations of love and goodness we are; and the unalterable truth that we are each a beautiful, precious child of God. Our hearts open to walk the way of love, leading us to a life of peace, serenity, and deep joy.

**Ponder:** Where do I need God's tender mercy? What dark areas of my life need God's light of love and truth? How can I learn to walk the way of love and peace?

**Prayer:** Lord, the light of your love dispels the darkness in my life. Wrap me in your love and tender care, and shine your light of truth upon me. Guide me on the way of love and peace.

**Practice:** Today I will be kind, patient, and gentle with everyone I encounter.

# Christmas

# Vigil Mass

*Isaiah 62:1–5*
*Psalm 89:4–5, 16–17, 27, 29*
*Acts 13:16–17, 22–25*
*Matthew 1:1–25*

"Joseph, son of David, do not be afraid to take Mary your wife into your home. For it is through the Holy Spirit that this child has been conceived in her."

**MATTHEW 1:20.**

**Reflection:** It is only right and just that Jesus receive special attention during the Christmas season. Christians throughout the world celebrate the birth of Jesus, the Son of God. We welcome Jesus, who is the visible presence of the God of love, peace, compassion, mercy, and justice.

As we celebrate the birth of Jesus, we must not overlook the Holy Spirit's important role in God's mysterious plan. It is by the power of the Holy Spirit that we are able to conceive and give birth to all that belongs to God. Christmas not only recalls the great event of the birth of Christ, it also reminds us of the presence and power of the Holy Spirit working in and through our lives.

Christmas is a time for every Christian to think about the ways in which he or she can give birth to God's love, peace, compassion, mercy, and justice in all the barren places where conflict, human destruction, violence, and war exist. Just as Mary offered her whole being and committed her life to being a servant of the incarnate Word, we must never be afraid to bring forth from the depths of our hearts the love, peace, and joy of God that the Holy Spirit has conceived in us.

*Ponder:* What is the true meaning of Christmas?

*Prayer:* Lord, you came into the world to reveal God's love, compassion, peace, mercy, and justice. May your Holy Spirit empower me to do the work of God without fear.

*Practice:* Today I will talk to someone about the true meaning of Christmas.

# Mass at Midnight

*Isaiah 9:1–6*
*Psalm 96:1–2, 2–3, 11–12, 13*
*Titus 2:11–14*
*Luke 2:1–14*

**The people who walked in darkness have seen a great light; Upon those who dwelt in the land of gloom a light has shone.**

ISAIAH 9:1

*Reflection:* We have to walk in the darkness of life before we can appreciate the gift and beauty of the light. In the darkness of pain and suffering, we await to be in the light of good health. In the darkness of a life-draining addiction, we await to be in the light of recovery. In the darkness of unemployment, we await to be in the light of having a meaningful job. In the darkness of anxiety and depression, we await to be in the light of mental health. In the darkness of misery and poverty, we await to be in the light of having food, water, and shelter. In the darkness of selfishness and greed, we await to be in the light of selflessness, compassion, and generosity.

Jesus is the great light of God who comes to all who live in the darkness of alienation, brokenness, and suffering. Christmas reawakens our imaginations to see the many ways in which Jesus lights a way, leading us out of our darkness to a place of peace and joy.

**Ponder:** What is the darkness that engulfs my life at the moment?

**Prayer:** Lord, you are the light of the world. Show me the way to freedom and truth so that I may find inner peace and rejoice in the land of the living.

**Practice:** Today I will visit someone I have neglected and bring this person joy.

# Mass at Dawn

*Isaiah 62:11–12*
*Psalm 97:1, 6, 11–12*
*Titus 3:4–7*
*Luke 2:15–20*

**And Mary kept all these things, reflecting on them in her heart.**

LUKE 2:19

***Reflection:*** The gods of the marketplace and the malls entice us all year long to shop and buy for Christmas. These gods work tirelessly to take over Christmas and give it their own spin. The gods of the marketplace and the malls don't want us to reflect on the deeper things of life.

The true meaning of Christmas is not found in the marketplace and malls but in the Word of God. We can reflect on Mary and the way in which she handled all that was going on in her young life. She remained faithful to herself, sorting out in her heart truth from fiction. She did not allow herself to be controlled or manipulated by other voices. Her only desire was to do God's will and to be God's servant in light of the truth revealed in her heart. Mary teaches us during the Christmas season to do our inner work and not to surrender our lives to the gods of the marketplace and malls who lure us into a state of mindlessness and addictive shopping.

The authentic Christian experiences Christmas in the sanctuary of the heart and not in the den of the marketplace and the malls. Christmas is about homecoming, entering our hearts where we ponder the true gift, Jesus, the Son of God.

**Ponder:** What is driving me into the marketplace and the malls?

**Prayer:** Lord, you choose to dwell and reveal yourself in my heart. Create a space within me so that I may ponder more deeply the meaning of the gift of your presence.

**Practice:** Today I will ask the people that I am with to share a thought on the meaning of Christmas before opening Christmas gifts.

# Mass During the Day

*Isaiah 52:7–10*
*Psalm 98:1, 2–3, 3–4, 5–6*
*Hebrews 1:1–6*
*John 1:1–18*

**In the beginning was the Word, and the Word was with God, and the Word was God. He was in the beginning with God.**

**JOHN 1:1–2**

*Reflection:* Our beginning point is with God. Everything begins with God. Life would be wonderful if we would only remember the beginning. All was with God and all comes from God and shall return to God. If we want to understand who we are and what our purpose is in life, we need to return to the source of our existence: the Word of God. We cannot exist apart from the Word of God. We cannot love apart from the Word of God. We cannot hope apart from the Word of God. We cannot believe apart from the Word of God. This is why it is so important for all Christians to meditate on the Word of God daily.

It is essential that the people of God whose mission it is to proclaim the Word of God devote more time and energy and resources to learning how to read and interpret the Word of God in the human condition. The gift that every Christian can give himself or herself is the gift of learning *lectio divina.* Through the steady reading and reflecting on the Word of God, the love, peace, and compassion of God will become flesh in the world. We must remember that we, too, were with God in the beginning. We were with the Word. Now we must become the Word for others.

**Ponder:** Why am I reluctant to read the Word of God and learn about lectio divina?

**Prayer:** Lord, you are the living Word of God who came to dwell in hearts of all people. Increase my desire and strengthen my will to know the Word of God and to live it in my life.

**Practice:** Today I will read John 1:1–18 as the grace before meal.

# December 26

## SAINT STEPHEN

*Acts 6:8–10; 7:54–59*
*Psalm 31:3cd–4, 6, 8ab, 16bc, 17*
*Matthew 10:17–22*

**Stephen, filled with grace and power, was working great wonders and signs among the people.**

**ACTS 6:8**

***Reflection:*** We are each filled with God's grace and the power to make a difference in the world. God's grace is in our knowledge that we are made in God's image of love and goodness. God's grace is in our desire to help those who are poor, frightened, ill, or discouraged. God's grace is in our commitment to forgive those who have hurt us, to make amends to those we have hurt, and to treat all those we encounter with love and respect.

We are powerful beings. We have the power to change our attitudes, behaviors, habits, actions, and words. We have the power to let go of negativity and choose a positive outlook. We have the power to say no to abuse, victimization, peer pressure, or dishonesty. We have the power to enjoy the companionship of the people we live, work, and play with. We have the power to receive and give love.

Our challenge and calling is to combine our personal power with the grace we have received from God and prove by our life example the wonder of God's love among us.

**Ponder:** Am I aware of God's grace and power within me? Where has God's grace touched my life?

**Prayer:** Lord, you share with me your abundant grace and power. Show me your will for me as I learn to do great wonders in small ways in my home and community.

**Practice:** Today I will show signs of love and peace to the people in my home.

# December 27

## SAINT JOHN THE EVANGELIST

---

*1 John 1:1–4*
*Psalm 97:1–2, 5–6, 11–12*
*John 20:1a, 2–8*

**On the first day of the week, Mary of Magdala came to the tomb early in the morning, while it was still dark, and saw the stone removed from the tomb.**

**JOHN 20:1–2**

*Reflection:* We are still in the dark if we try to understand Christmas outside the event of the Resurrection. The fact that Jesus rose from the tomb helps us to see more clearly the significance of the Christmas event. If Jesus did not die and rise from the dead, Christmas would have no meaning for us.

Our Christian tradition is rooted in the truth that Jesus is the Son of God who was born, suffered death, was buried, and rose on the third day in accordance with the Scriptures. The Christmas event and the Easter event illuminate the core of our faith: Jesus is human and divine. Jesus came to share in our humanity so that we could become divine and live in communion with the triune God.

The Feast of St. John the Evangelist is celebrated in the Christmas season to remind all Christians of their call and responsibility to give witness to Jesus, who is, as our Creed proclaims: "God from God, Light from Light, true God from true God." We give witness to Jesus, the light to all people, who overcame the darkness of death and reigns forever as the light of the world.

**Ponder:** How can I be a witness to Jesus, the light of all people, to others?

Lord, your birth and resurrection reveal the power of God in the world. Illuminate my mind to understand more deeply the purpose and meaning of your life.

**Practice:** Today I will be Christ-like: a positive and hopeful presence to others.

# December 28

## HOLY INNOCENTS

---

*1 John 1:5—2:2*
*Psalm 124:2–3, 4–5, 7cd–8*
*Matthew 2:13–18*

**"Rise, take the child and his mother, flee to Egypt, and stay there until I tell you. Herod is going to search for the child to destroy him."**

**MATTHEW 2:13**

*Reflection:* There are some in our world who are searching for ways to create life, control and manipulate life, and fashion life according to their own ideas. There are some in our world who want to disclaim the fact that there is a God who governs and rules over all of creation. We can never allow anyone to usurp the role of God and dictate the terms of life. God is the source of all life. We believe that all life—from the womb to the tomb—is sacred and precious. We must do all that we can to protect the sanctity of human life and the dignity of the human person. These two universal principles ought to inform and guide everything we undertake in life. We must never lose sight of these principles because they shape our decisions to defend life, to help those who are refugees and exiles, those who suffer from famine, those unjustly deprived of liberty, those who are in prison, sick, and dying, and anyone whose life is being threatened to be destroyed by external forces. As Christians we are called to protect Jesus, who lives in every person and is one with all of humanity.

**Ponder:** What more can I do to defend the sanctity of life and the dignity of the human person?

**Prayer:** Lord, you are the source and giver of all life. May your Spirit strengthen my resolve to speak in defense of life from the womb to the tomb.

**Practice:** Today I will find a way to express my support for life.

# December 29

## FIFTH DAY IN THE OCTAVE OF CHRISTMAS

---

*1 John 2:3–11*
*Psalm 96:1–2a, 2b–3, 5b–6*
*Luke 2:22–35*

**This is the way we may know that we are in union with him: whoever claims to abide in him ought to live (just) as he lived.**

**1 JOHN 2:5–6**

*Reflection:* If we do not base all that we are in awareness of God's love for each and every member of the human family, then we are not walking as Jesus walked.

To become aware of God's love for us personally is where our walk begins. We cultivate this awareness by spending quiet time seeking God's presence. This may be in the form of a meditation where we sit in stillness and empty our minds of thought; in a written prayer where we pour out our anxieties and longings to God; in seeking spiritual guidance from someone we trust; or in absorbing the beauty and wonder of nature and knowing God as Creator.

As we begin to walk with the awareness of God's presence and love for us personally, we find this new awareness begins to change how we see and treat others. We can no longer be indifferent to the pain and suffering of others. We seek ways to be a healing presence for others, and our walk becomes more and more like the walk of Jesus.

**Ponder:** How can I become more aware of God's presence in my life? Whom do I see when I look at other people?

**Prayer:** Lord, you walk in communion with all of humanity. Open my eyes, ears, mind, and heart to your presence. Heal whatever prevents me from knowing you are with me and love me. Teach me to love others as you love me.

**Practice:** Today I will seek to improve my conscious contact with God through a ten-minute meditation.

# December 30

## SIXTH DAY IN THE OCTAVE OF CHRISTMAS

---

*1 John 2:12–17*
*Psalm 96:7–8a, 8b–9, 10*
*Luke 2:36–40*

**There was also a prophetess, Anna, the daughter of Phanuel, of the tribe of Asher. She was advanced in years, having lived seven years with her husband after her marriage, and then as a widow until she was eighty-four.**

**LUKE 2:36–37**

*Reflection:* Age has nothing to do with our relationship with God. We are made in the image of God's love and goodness. We are in God and God is in us from the beginning to eternity. We are beloved of God at all times, forever.

The physical changes that aging brings can undermine our sense of self-worth. Our smooth skin becomes wrinkled. We move more slowly and tire more quickly. Our bones become more fragile and we may become more susceptible to illness. We think because we are frail, we are less useful. We think because we are less energetic, we are less enjoyable to be around. We think because we are wrinkled, we are less beautiful. We are so wrapped up in our physical self that we forget the beauty of our inner love and goodness.

We must remember that at any age our love and goodness are blessings to others. The world is richer because of our love and goodness. We touch hearts and bring healing with our love and goodness. We show others the face of God with our love and goodness, and our love and goodness allow us to see the face of God in others.

*Ponder:* Who are the wise elders in my life? Do I still feel useful and productive in life?

*Prayer:* Lord, all human life is a gift from you. Help me to age gracefully and to respect those who are my elders.

*Practice:* Today I will visit someone at a local senior center or nursing home.

# December 31

## SEVENTH DAY IN THE OCTAVE OF CHRISTMAS

---

*1 John 2:18–21*
*Psalm 96:1–2, 11–12, 13*
*John 1:1–18*

**In the beginning was the Word, and the Word was with God, and the Word was God. And the Word became flesh and made his dwelling among us.**

**JOHN 1:1, 14**

*Reflection:* God speaks to us through the life and example of Jesus, who shows us the way of love, compassion, and forgiveness. Jesus, God's Word made flesh, is our teacher, companion, and spiritual guide as we struggle to walk the way of love.

Whenever we are in difficulty or have a problem that is causing us anxiety, taking the time to open our Bible and read God's precious Word brings us new insights and takes us in new directions. When we feel stuck, hopeless, unloved, or confused, a few minutes spent with the Word brings a feeling of closeness to God. We realize we are not alone. We open our hearts to God's healing presence and let go of our need to fuss and worry. We find hope again and the faith to keep on living.

Throughout Scripture, God tells us: Do not be afraid. The Word of God is reassuring, comforting, and loving. The Word of God also challenges us to move beyond our fears to love deeply, generously, and wholeheartedly.

**Ponder:** When do I spend time with the Word of God? How does the Word of God speak to me? How is my life changed by the Word of God?

**Prayer:** Lord, your Word is eternal, dynamic, and gives meaning to my life. Increase my desire to spend time with you in sacred Scripture.

**Practice:** Today I will read a passage from my favorite book of the Bible and reflect on it throughout the day.

# January 1

## MARY, MOTHER OF GOD

---

*Numbers 6:22–27*
*Psalm 67:2–3, 5, 6, 8*
*Galatians 4:4–7*
*Luke 2:16–21*

As proof that you are children, God sent the spirit of his Son into our hearts, crying out, "Abba, Father!" So you are no longer a slave but a child, and if a child then also an heir, through God.

**GALATIANS 4:6–7**

**Reflection:** It is difficult for most Christians to wrap their minds around the thought that every person is a child of God. If the Spirit of God's Son is in our hearts, this means that we are all sons and daughters of God, members of God's family. This truth changes the way we look at people and treat them. With the Spirit of God's Son in us, we are challenged to see every person as a sacred dwelling place of God. When we encounter another person we must remember that we are encountering God. If we approached every person with this understanding, we would be more respectful and caring in our interactions with others. We would be more accepting, less critical and judgmental of others.

When Mary accepted the invitation to be the Mother of God, she also accepted God's plan to make every person an adopted son and daughter. It is hard to imagine that we are part of a cosmic family made up of people from all over the world and all walks of life. We need to think about Mary, the Mother of God, about her trust, openness, and courage in accepting God's plan. We are the adopted sons and daughters of God. It is time for us to open our hearts, to trust, and to be courageous enough to live in peace and love with all people.

**Ponder:** What am I resolved to do to live in peace and love with others?

**Prayer:** Lord, your Spirit has been poured into my heart, making me a child of God. Help me to see every person as my brother and sister, and show deep respect and love.

**Practice:** Today I will discern more carefully my New Year's resolutions.

# January 2

*1 John 2:22–28*
*Psalm 98:1, 2–3ab, 3cd–4*
*John 1:19–28*

**"There is one among you whom you do not recognize."**

*Reflection:* We think we know others. We think we know what makes them tick, what they like and dislike, what will make them happy, sad, or angry. Sometimes we make judgments about others based on what we know. We judge them as stupid, quick-tempered, oversensitive, or fussy. These labels give us the illusion that we are able to control others through our judgment of them.

Our need to control others is an expression of fear. We are afraid of the unknown and unexplored spiritual power of ourselves and others. We are afraid of the power of love.

God's example of unconditional love teaches us that all people must be free to be fully themselves, with all their human strengths and weaknesses. Love is a willingness to step into the unknown without preconceived notions. Love is diving into the mystery of each person and enjoying what we find without trying to change or distort it.

Accepting that each of us is created in the image of God's love and goodness is all we need to recognize that God is among us.

**Ponder:** When have I experienced the mystery of another? When have I touched my own mystery?

**Prayer:** Lord, your love helps me to embrace the unknown. Reveal yourself to me so that I may recognize you in myself and others.

**Practice:** Today I will be careful not to judge anyone.

# January 3

*1 John 2:29—3:6*
*Psalm 98:1, 3cd–4, 5–6*
*John 1:29–34*

**See what love the Father has bestowed on us that we may be called the children of God. Yet so we are.**

1 JOHN 3:1

*Reflection:* The whole of the human family is our family because we are all children of God. God delights in us and watches over each of us with tender, gentle, and unconditional love. God encourages us to explore our heritage of love and goodness, and gives us Jesus to be our teacher. In our imitation of Jesus, we learn to share our experience of love, compassion, and forgiveness with all those we encounter.

Along with physical, mental, and emotional maturing comes spiritual maturing. We learn to discern our gifts and talents and to make good use of them in continuing the good work of love. We learn to act consciously, choosing to respond with respect and love to others rather than react impulsively. We learn to nurture ourselves by seeking the companionship of God through prayer, meditation, and reading of the Scriptures.

With all that we know and experience, we are still children in our spirituality. We will always have something to learn. We will always have growing to do. We will always need the support of our human family. We will always rely on God's love and guidance.

*Ponder:* Do I possess childlike innocence? How have I matured spiritually? What is my image of God?

*Prayer:* Lord, you are my hope and strength. Teach me humility so that I may keep learning and growing spiritually.

*Practice:* Today I will get in touch with my inner child.

# January 4

*1 John 3:7–10*
*Psalm 98:1, 7–8, 9*
*John 1:35–42*

[Jesus] said to them, "What are you looking for?" They said to him, "Rabbi" (which translated means Teacher), "where are you staying?" He said to them, "Come, and you will see."

JOHN 1:38–39

***Reflection:*** We are all looking for reassurance that our lives are meaningful and we are loved. Yet we do not always hear the invitation to come and see where Jesus—the one who gives meaning and purpose to our lives and the one who loves us unconditionally—dwells.

We are accustomed to looking outside ourselves to find God. We point to the sky and talk about heaven. We go to church and think God is caged in the tabernacle. We do good works and look for God's face in others.

It is right to look for God in others; it is also right to look for God in ourselves. Jesus dwells in our hearts, guiding us, teaching us, loving us. Our hearts are not mere physical pumps. Our hearts hold our instincts, our intuition, our sense of right and wrong, our sense of justice, our compassion.

Jesus invites us to come and see our inner truth. He invites us to shine the light of love on our lives so that we might let go of all the dark obstacles—shame, rage, arrogance, prejudice, fear—that prevent us from knowing the purity of our hearts.

**Ponder:** What do I hold in my heart?

**Prayer:** Lord, you search me and know me. Give me the courage to sit still and look in my own heart to find you.

**Practice:** Today I will spend ten minutes alone in a quiet place with nothing to distract me from listening to the inner voice of my heart.

# January 5

*1 John 3:11–21*
*Psalm 100:1b–2, 3, 4, 5*
*John 1:43–51*

**For this is the message you have heard from the beginning: we should love one another.**

**1 JOHN 3:11**

*Reflection:* Love is what our lives are all about. Our purpose is to love one another.

We don't automatically know how to love. Love is something we learn. If we were brought up by people who never learned how to love, we will have to find our teachers elsewhere. If our family showed us love only when they approved of our behavior, we will have to learn how to love unconditionally and consistently. If people said they loved us and then disrespected our being, we will have to heal the shame and learn to let go of our confusion about love.

Love is not only about romance or good feelings. Love is respect for others. Love is encouraging the discouraged. Love is praying for our enemies. Love is letting go of the need to be right.

Love is paying attention. Love is listening deeply. Love is sharing our mental, physical, emotional, and spiritual resources. Love is discerning our gifts and talents and using them in service to others. Love is letting others be themselves without interfering.

We are called to love. Love is our purpose and our joy. Love is our beginning, and with love there is no end.

**Ponder:** How do I express love? Whom do I find hard to love? Do I trust God's love for me?

**Prayer:** Lord, you commanded us to love God, ourselves, and our neighbors. Help me to let go of my fear of love. Show me how to set my heart free to love as you did.

**Practice:** Today I will practice love by paying attention when people speak to me.

# Epiphany of the Lord

*Isaiah 60:1–6*
*Psalm 72:1–2, 7–8, 10–11, 12–13*
*Ephesians 3:2–3a, 5–6*
*Matthew 2:1–12*

**Rise up in splendor! Your light has come, the glory of the LORD shines upon you. See, darkness covers the earth, and thick clouds cover the peoples; But upon you the LORD shines, and over you appears his glory.**

**ISAIAH 60:1–2**

*Reflection:* Each day is an Epiphany. We live in the light of God, who created us. We are redeemed in the light of Jesus who poured out his life for the sake of sinful humanity. We are empowered to be the light of God for others by the gift of the Holy Spirit. Each day is an opportunity to open our hearts to let the light of God shine through us. Our light shines brightly when we choose to celebrate life, to share goodness, compassion, peace, and love with others.

Epiphany means living in the light of God and bringing the light of God to all the dark places in our families, communities, nation, and the world. Epiphany challenges every Christian to be the light of love to unloving people; the light of forgiveness in unforgiving situations; the light of kindness in a climate of incivility; and the light of understanding in the face of invincible ignorance. We are the glory of God in the world. We are the epiphanies that can make a difference in people's lives.

**Ponder:** Where do I need to let my light shine?

**Prayer:** Lord, your light gives us strength and shows us the way to God. Remove my blindness that I may see the light of goodness, peace, and love within myself and others.

**Practice:** Today I will have a positive attitude and look for the good in others.

# Feast Days

# Immaculate Conception of the Blessed Virgin Mary

(December 8; December 9 if
December 8 is a Sunday)

*Genesis 3:9–15, 20*
*Psalm 98: 1, 2–3, 3–4*
*Ephesians 1:3–6, 11–12*
*Luke 1:26–38*

**[Gabriel] said, "Hail, favored one! The Lord is with you."**

LUKE 1:28

**Reflection:** God loves us perfectly, unconditionally, joyfully, and without end. God is with us, in our mind, our heart, our every cell. We are called to bring God to our families, friends, and enemies.

God asks if we are ready to give God's love to the world. We can say no; God will not reject us. God will gently lead us to a place where we feel safe and fearless and ready to say yes to love and peace.

*Ponder:* How do I bring love and peace to my life?

*Prayer:* Lord, here I am. You have made me available for your purpose in the world. Show me how to bring your love and peace to my daily life.

*Practice:* Today I volunteer my time and talent to a church or community project.

# Holy Family of Jesus, Mary, and Joseph

## YEAR A

*Sirach 3:2–7, 12–14*
*Psalm 128:1–2, 3, 4–5*
*Colossians 3:12–21*
*Matthew 2:13–15, 19–23*

Bearing with one another and forgiving one another, if one has a grievance against another; as the Lord has forgiven you, so must you also do. And over all these put on love, that is, the bond of perfection.

COLOSSIANS 3:13–14)

*Reflection:* We recognize a person's profession by the uniform he or she wears. We recognize law enforcement officials by their uniform. We recognize nurses and doctors by their uniform. We recognize sports teams by their uniform. It is not always so easy to recognize a Christian because a Christian is identified by the inner clothing of the heart. We cannot see another person's heart, but we can sense what is in the heart through a person's actions. The universal clothing of the Christian heart is love and forgiveness. The family unit is the school of love and forgiveness, the foundation of our society, and a model of the Church. What is learned or not learned in the family influences our moral and spiritual development, inter-personal relationships, and social behavior. It is difficult to create a loving, forgiving community, society, church, and world when families have neglected to teach their children how to love and forgive at home. We can recognize a Christian family by the way people love and forgive one another.

**Ponder:** What have I learned from my family?

**Prayer:** Lord, you teach me the importance of family life. Keep my family in peace and deepen my love, respect, and appreciation for all the members of my family.

**Practice:** Today, I will say I'm sorry to someone I have hurt.

# YEAR B

*Genesis 15:1–6; 21:1–3*
*Psalm 105:1–2, 3–4, 5–6, 8–9*
*Hebrews 11:8, 11–12, 17–19*
*Luke 2:22–40*

**The child grew and became strong, filled with wisdom; and the favor of God was upon him.**

**LUKE 2:40**

***Reflection:*** Some people say our children and youth are growing up too fast. Most are not adequately equipped to deal with the real world. They lack critical thinking skills to discern what is important in life. They are emotionally immature, finding it difficult to have meaningful relationships. They are spiritual seekers, lacking spiritual depth and guidance. They are addicted to technology, disinterested and detached from nature. They eat fast food, becoming obese and unhealthy. They want independence, unable to move on with their lives. They want unbridled freedom, making bad decisions that further complicate their lives.

Our children and youth cannot grow and mature without being rooted in a loving family with clear moral principles, spiritual values, and a deep self-knowledge. God's love is upon all our children and youth. It is the responsibility of every Christian family to show our children and youth how to grow in love, be strong in love, and be filled with the wisdom of God's love. Life for our children and youth can be a good experience when they slow down and learn how to love God and neighbor.

*Ponder:* What are our children and youth learning about life?

*Prayer:* Lord, Mary and Joseph helped you to grow in love and wisdom. Surround me with loving and caring people to help me to be a wise, loving, and caring person.

*Practice:* Today I will research ways I can help children and youth in my community.

# YEAR C

---

*1 Samuel 1:20–22, 24–28*
*Psalm 84:2–3, 5–6, 9–10*
*1 John 3:1–2, 21–24*
*Luke 2:41–52*

**After three days they found him in the temple, sitting in the midst of the teachers, listening to them and asking them questions, and all who heard him were astounded at his understanding and his answers.**

LUKE 2:46–47

*Reflection:* Where can we go to have a conversation on some of the important issues facing us today, such as: the nature and meaning of life, human dignity, respect for others, care for creation, family life, human rights, fair trade, economic justice, universal peace, interreligious dialogue, and human development? Some Christians are not aware that the Church has rich social teachings that address these and other issues facing our society and world. Some Christians are not aware of the wisdom contained in these teachings and how they can help us to respond with an enlightened perspective to those who are searching for answers to today's challenges.

Parents are the primary educators of their children in the way of faith and morals. As members of God's family—the Church—parents need to learn more about the social teachings of the Church and be able to share this wisdom with their children and youth. Parents will be pleasantly amazed and astonished at the wealth of this wisdom.

**Ponder:** What do I know about the social teachings of the Church?

**Prayer:** Lord, through your Word we receive the knowledge and wisdom of God. May your Spirit lead me to your sacred Word and guide me in my search for knowledge and truth.

**Practice:** Today I will make the effort to become familiar with the social teachings of the Catholic Church.